FORD MUSTANG
SHELBY GT350

BY EMILY ROSE OACHS

™

Are you ready to take it to the extreme?
Torque books thrust you into the action-packed world
of sports, vehicles, mystery, and adventure. These books
may include dirt, smoke, fire, and dangerous stunts.
WARNING: read at your own risk.

This edition first published in 2017 by Bellwether Media, Inc.

No part of this publication may be reproduced in whole or in part without written permission of the publisher.
For information regarding permission, write to Bellwether Media, Inc., Attention: Permissions Department,
5357 Penn Avenue South, Minneapolis, MN 55419.

Library of Congress Cataloging-in-Publication Data

Names: Oachs, Emily Rose, author.
Title: Ford Mustang Shelby GT350 / by Emily Rose Oachs.
Other titles: Car Crazy (Minneapolis, Minn.)
Description: Minneapolis, MN : Bellwether Media, Inc., 2017. | Series:
   Torque: Car Crazy | Audience: Ages 7-12. | Includes bibliographical
   references and index.
Identifiers: LCCN 2016037684 (print) | LCCN 2016046117 (ebook) | ISBN
   9781626175792 (hardcover : alk. paper) | ISBN 9781681033082 (ebook)
Subjects: LCSH: Mustang automobile–Juvenile literature.
Classification: LCC TL215.M8 O23 2016 (print) | LCC TL215.M8 (ebook) | DDC
   629.222/2-dc23
LC record available at https://lccn.loc.gov/2016037684

Editor: Betsy Rathburn   Designer: Brittany McIntosh

Printed in the United States of America, North Mankato, MN.

TABLE OF
CONTENTS

HIGH-POWERED PERFORMANCE

A winding road twists through the countryside. On it, a Ford Mustang Shelby GT350 speeds around the curves. This **pony car** handles the tight turns gracefully.

A steep hill appears ahead. The engine easily carries the car up and over it.

PONY CARS EARNED THEIR NAME FROM THE FORD MUSTANG. IT WAS THE FIRST POPULAR PONY CAR EVER BUILT!

On a **straightaway**, the Mustang Shelby GT350 lets loose. The driver presses the pedal to the floor. The engine roars as the car **accelerates**. Nothing can beat this pony car's performance!

THE HISTORY OF FORD

Henry Ford

As a young man, Henry Ford loved to work with machines. He completed his first automobile in 1896. Seven years later, Henry started the Ford Motor Company.

The famous Ford **Model** T came out in 1908. Its popularity boomed! To meet demand, Henry created the **assembly line**. It helped workers build cars faster at a lower cost. As a result, car prices dropped. More people could afford to buy Ford cars!

1925 Ford
Model T

MILLIONS MADE
FORD STOPPED MAKING THE MODEL T IN 1927. BY THEN, THE COMPANY HAD BUILT 15 MILLION MODEL T CARS!

Henry began opening factories in countries around the world. By 1921, more than half of the cars on American roads were made by Ford. Since then, Ford has introduced many successful cars, trucks, and sport utility vehicles (SUVs).

Ford assembly line

WHAT'S IN A NAME?

NOBODY KNOWS WHERE THE MUSTANG GOT ITS NAME. SOME CLAIM IT CAME FROM A WORLD WAR II FIGHTER AIRPLANE. OTHERS SAY IT CAME FROM THE HORSE.

1965 Ford Mustang

In 1964, the company introduced the first Mustang. Fans quickly fell in love with the car's style, power, and price. Today, Ford still makes some of the most popular

FORD MUSTANG SHELBY GT350

In the 1960s, Ford teamed up with the American car racer Carroll Shelby. Carroll designed a Mustang for the racetrack.

The first Ford Mustang Shelby GT350 was built in 1964. Fans loved the more powerful Mustang. Ford continued to make the Mustang Shelby GT350 until 1969. But the company announced the car's return in 2014!

1965 Ford Mustang Shelby GT350

DESIGNING CHAMPIONS

CARROLL ALSO DEVELOPED FORD'S GT40 CARS. IN 1966, THEY WERE THE TOP THREE CARS IN THE 24 HOURS OF LE MANS RACE!

TECHNOLOGY AND GEAR

A Mustang Shelby GT350's **V8 engine** springs to life at the touch of a button. The car can accelerate up to 175 miles (282 kilometers) per hour!

Powerful brakes quickly bring the speedy car to safe stops. On corners, a special **suspension system** constantly adjusts to road conditions. This gives the car the best **handling** possible.

V8 engine

fender
vent

rear diffuser

The Mustang Shelby GT350 was designed for the track. Features on its body make the car as fast and powerful as possible.

Fat tires help the car grip the road. On the sides, **fender** vents allow hot air from the engine to escape. A lowered hood and **rear diffuser** make the car more **aerodynamic**.

CELEBRITY COLLECTION

FORMER HOST OF *THE TONIGHT SHOW* JAY LENO IS FAMOUS FOR HIS CAR COLLECTION. HE OWNS A 2015 MUSTANG SHELBY GT350R. ONLY 37 WERE BUILT THAT YEAR!

The Mustang Shelby GT350's inside is as sporty as its outside. Race car seats hold the driver and passengers in place. Behind the wheel, a display tracks the car's acceleration and speed.

Five driving modes allow drivers to change the car's performance. They control the Mustang Shelby GT350's steering, **traction**, and power.

2017 FORD MUSTANG SHELBY GT350 SPECIFICATIONS

CAR STYLE	COUPE
ENGINE	5.2L V8
TOP SPEED	175 MILES (282 KILOMETERS) PER HOUR
0 - 60 TIME	4.3 SECONDS
HORSEPOWER	526 HP (392 KILOWATTS) @7,500 RPM
CURB WEIGHT	3,760 POUNDS (1,706 KILOGRAMS)
WIDTH	81.9 INCHES (208 CENTIMETERS)
LENGTH	189.6 INCHES (482 CENTIMETERS)
HEIGHT	54.2 INCHES (138 CENTIMETERS)
WHEEL SIZE	19 INCHES (48 CENTIMETERS)
COST	STARTS AT $54,570

TODAY AND THE FUTURE

The Ford Mustang Shelby GT350 returned 50 years after the original. Like the first **generation**, it continues to rule both the road and track. Its powerful engine and smooth ride make the Shelby GT350 the leader of the pony car pack!

THREE-BAR TAILLIGHTS   **FENDER VENTS**   **HOOD VENT**

GLOSSARY

accelerates—increases in speed

aerodynamic—having a shape that can move through air quickly

assembly line—a series of workers who each do a specific task to put together an item

fender—metal that curves around a car's wheels to stop rocks and dirt from flying into the air

generation—a version of the same model

handling—how a car performs around turns

model—a specific kind of car

pony car—a stylish, high-performance car that is affordably priced

rear diffuser—a part on the back underside of a car that directs air and makes the car more aerodynamic

straightaway—the straight part of a track or road

suspension system—a series of springs and shocks that help a car grip the road

traction—the force that helps a car grip the road

V8 engine—an engine with 8 cylinders arranged in the shape

TO LEARN MORE

AT THE LIBRARY

Blackford, Cheryl. *Powerful Muscle Cars.* North Mankato, Minn.: Capstone Press, 2015.

Hamilton, John. *Muscle Cars.* Minneapolis, Minn.: ABDO Pub., 2013.

Piddock, Charles. *Ford Mustang.* Vero Beach, Fla.: Rourke Educational Media, 2016.

ON THE WEB

Learning more about the Ford Mustang Shelby GT350 is as easy as 1, 2, 3.

1. Go to www.factsurfer.com.

2. Enter "Ford Mustang Shelby GT350" into the search box.

3. Click the "Surf" button and you will see a list of related web sites.

With factsurfer.com, finding more information is just a click away.

INDEX

The images in this book are reproduced through the courtesy of: THE FORD MOTOR COMPANY, front cover, pp. 4-5, 6-7, 14, 15 (top, bottom), 16 (top, bottom), 17, 18, 19, 20-21, 21 (top left, top center, top right); Photo Researchers, Inc/ Alamy, p. 8; Stocksearch/ Alamy, p. 9; Sueddeutsche Zeitung Photo/ Alamy, p. 10; Ollieholmes, p. 11; Oleksiy Maksymenko Photography/ Alamy, p. 12; AP Images, p. 13 (top); Goddard Automotive/ Alamy, p. 13 (bottom).